great
party
dips

great party dips

peggy fallon

photography by
alexandra grablewski

WILEY

JOHN WILEY & SONS, INC.

This book is printed on acid-free paper.
Copyright © 2009 by King Hill Productions. All rights reserved
Photography copyright 2009 by Alexandra Grablewski
Book design by Elizabeth Van Itallie
Food styling by Brian Preston-Campbell
Prop styling by Barb Fritz

Published by John Wiley & Sons, Inc., Hoboken, New Jersey
Published simultaneously in Canada

For general information on our other products and services or for technical support,
please contact our Customer Care Department within the United States at (800) 762-
2974, outside the United States at (317) 572-3993 or fax (317) 572-4002.

Wiley also publishes its books in a variety of electronic formats. Some content that
appears in print may not be available in electronic books. For more information about
Wiley products, visit our web site at www.wiley.com.

Library of Congress Cataloging-in-Publication Data:

Fallon, Peggy.
 Great party dips / Peggy Fallon ; photography by Alexandra Grablewski.
    p. cm.
 Includes index.
 ISBN 978-0-470-23978-0 (cloth : alk. paper)
 1. Dips (Appetizers) 2. Appetizers. I. Title.
 TX740.F35 2008
 641.8'12--dc22

                              2008007627

Printed in China

10 9 8 7 6 5 4 3 2 1

for joseph, noah, and eli—
my favorite little dippers.

contents

acknowledgments

Many thanks to Justin Schwartz at John Wiley & Sons for sharing my enthusiasm in this project. Sincere gratitude also goes to Linda Gollober for her meticulous recipe testing; to Patricia Stapley, Beth Hensperger, Moira Bromham, and all the other friends who shared their favorite recipes as well as their opinions; and especially to Susan Wyler, wordsmith extraordinaire.

introduction

not just the same old dips

Culinary trends come and go like any other fashion, but some forms of entertaining never lose their appeal. Whether the tone you're seeking is penthouse posh or backyard casual, classic or contemporary, American or international, dips remain one of the simplest—and most popular—appetizers on the party scene. That's because unlike individual savory pastries and other finger food, which take an inordinate amount of time and effort, a wide array of interesting dips and spreads can be whipped up in no time. All you have to learn is how to present them beautifully.

Dips and spreads can be as humble as a ceramic crock of blended cheeses or as elegant as a creamy crab dip warmed in a silver chafing dish. Plain or fancy, these one-bowl appetizers are quick and easy to make. They also offer an amazing range of styles and flavors that appeal to every palate: creamy, hot, tart, spicy, rich, salty, sweet, and herbaceous.

Contemporary ingredients and new ethnic flavors—like smoked paprika, Asian fish sauce, tamarind paste, pomegranate molasses, pedigreed olive oils, various chiles, and a multitude of fine vinegars—offer fresh ways to whip up food for fashionable entertaining. Favored international tastes that have become familiar—such as Indian, Thai, and, of course, Mexican—add greatly to the repertoire of traditional American standards and popular Italian and Mediterranean flavors. There's also the appeal of the textural contrast between a soft, unctuous dip and the crisp vegetables or chips that feel so satisfying when you crunch down on them. Best of all, dips and spreads are "self-serve." You simply put them out and walk away. Guests help themselves, and you are free to enjoy the party.

Whether you're offering a dip before a meal or the dips and

spreads are the meal—in the case of a cocktail party—this collection of recipes gives you plenty to choose from: hot, cold, and in-between. While many classic dips are based on mayonnaise, sour cream, or cream cheese, many here also feature olive oil, vegetables, beans, and other less conventional foundations to make lighter, leaner dips. The salsas are by and large colorful, low in fat, and bright in flavor.

Most of these recipes are so simple that even a novice cook can pass for a pro. At the same time, dips and spreads provide respite for the passionate cook who is busy preparing the rest of the meal or who is searching for something fast and fabulous to bring to a potluck or office party. Children can whip up their favorite dipping snack with little or no supervision; dips are by far the best way to entice kids to eat vegetables.

Beyond offering a medley of choices for any cocktail party, dips and spreads serve well as light and easy before-dinner offerings to whet the appetite; as a satisfying late-afternoon or late-evening snack; or as a great way to curl up in front of a wide-screen TV. What would Super Sunday football or an Oscar party be without big bowls of dips and chips?

presentation, presentation, presentation

Because dips and spreads are by their nature so unpretentious, most benefit from even the simplest decoration, like a sprinkling of bright red paprika on a bowl of beige hummus or a few green sprigs of fresh thyme or dill atop a brown pâté. After all, first impressions count, and it's so easy to enhance eye appeal.

Begin by choosing the right container, considering both size and color. I like to allow about one inch of space below the rim of the bowl for both practical reasons and visual interest. Too little dip in too large a bowl will look skimpy and be hard to navigate. If filled to the brim, you lose the contrast between bowl and dip, which looks ungainly and most likely will get messy as soon as the first guest dips in.

A dark-colored bowl can set off a light dip, or a brightly colored pattern on a Spanish or Italian dish can add visual interest to a bland-looking spread. Very thick dips, such as Guacamole with Jalapeño and Lime (page 29), can be mounded directly onto a platter and rounded into a dome shape with a flexible metal spatula, then garnished as you like.

It's also fun to think outside the box. A dip doesn't have to go in a bowl; it can be mounded in a large martini glass or small stemmed compote, or used to fill an unconventional container, like a flower pot or children's toy, lined with plastic wrap. Seldom-used kitchen equipment, like small terrines or old copper molds, can be used for spreads and pâtés. Old baskets and wooden bowls are wonderful for chips; a Chinese bamboo steamer makes the perfect container for Won Ton Crisps (page 121). For warm dips, a fondue pot, small chafing dish, or electric dipping pot is nice to keep hot dips warm and melted cheese gooey.

Large vegetables can be hollowed out and used either by themselves or as holders for a hidden bowl of dip. For example, split a bright bell pepper lengthwise, remove the seeds, and you've got a perfect container to hold small portions of dips or spreads. For a striking presentation, a bowl of dip can be nestled in a hollowed-out red cabbage or turban squash.

Spreads and pâtés can be dabbed onto the end of Belgian endive spears and arranged geometrically or in a spoke pattern on a round platter, which ends up looking like a flower. Or they can be used to fill gougères, tiny pastry shells, hollowed-out cherry tomatoes, cooked new potato halves, or cucumber cups.

Set out your appetizers strategically. If it's a larger party and you're offering an assortment of dips and spreads, make sure there's no line to get at the chips. Try to place the dips and their appropriate dunkers around the room rather than grouping them all in one place.

Finally, consider your garnish. It should be edible, and contemporary style dictates that it also should relate to one of the ingredients in the dish. No strawberries or orange wedges perched atop a bean dip these days. A sprig of fresh herb, a dusting of paprika, or a few chopped nuts scattered on top is all you need. After all, as soon as a couple of people have dipped in, it will all be gone anyway.

dip arithmetic

Wherever possible, recipes in this book contain both a cup-measure yield and the number of people the dip or spread serves. This is meant to be helpful, but keep in mind it is only a guideline. If you put out two dips that each serve 6 to 8, together they might serve 10 to 12 rather than 12 to 16. In general, the more food you offer, the more people will eat. Also remember that luxury ingredients like crab and shrimp are usually consumed with more gusto than everyday foods.

Yields also depend upon what food you are serving; how filling the dippers are; whether the party is in the daytime or evening; whether it's a casual or formal affair; whether it's a two-hour cocktail party or an all-night bash; whether the guests are all male, female, or a mixed group; whether alcohol is being consumed; and on and on.

When offering a little something before a dinner party, a single dip or spread along with some olives and nuts is more than enough. For a two-hour cocktail party, as a general rule, professional caterers generally allow 10 to 12 "pieces" per guest. This refers to canapés and other pickup appetizers or to 3 to 4 tablespoons of dip. Of course, as the number of guests increases, so should the menu, because you want variety as well as quantity and a pleasing mix of flavors, colors, and textures.

On the other hand, if you're hunkering down alone in front of the television with a big bowl of Caramelized Onion Dip (page 31) and a giant bag of potato chips, the word "calorie" will probably slip from your brain, and with no one else in sight, the food will disappear as if by magic. At least that's the case at my house.

crudités and other dunkers

For dipping, I almost always like to offer crudités as well as chips, because the cut-up raw and lightly blanched vegetables are colorful as well as light and nutritious. These used to be a lot of work, but in addition to baby carrots, supermarkets now offer a wide range of vegetables already cut up, which saves a lot of time and trouble.

Crudités often form the most strikingly beautiful part of the appetizer table. They can be arranged flat on a platter, with attention to adjacent contrasts of color, or standing up in deep baskets or unconventional containers. Leafy liners of ruffled lettuce or raw kale are optional. Tip: Place a small ice pack in the base of your crudité basket or other container to prevent the vegetables from wilting during the party.

A large number of vegetables are simply perfect served au naturel (i.e., raw); others benefit from blanching for a minute or two to brighten their appearance and tenderize them slightly.

To blanch vegetables, bring a large pot of salted water to a boil. Add a large handful of vegetables (only one variety at a time). As soon as the water returns to a boil, lift out the vegetables with a strainer or spoon and immediately plunge them into a large bowl of ice water. Firmer vegetables, like green beans, may require an extra minute or two. If tiny new potatoes are part of your crudité basket, they should of course be fully cooked until tender. Serve at once or wrap in paper towels and refrigerate in zipper-seal plastic bags. They'll keep for at least a day.

If blanching a large variety of vegetables, you can use the same water to blanch them all. Just remember to begin with the milder vegetables, such as snow peas and green beans, and progress to the stronger ones, like broccoli and cauliflower, so their flavors remain distinct.

vegetables best eaten raw

- Frozen artichoke hearts, thawed and well drained
- Belgian endive leaves
- Bell peppers
- Carrots
- Celery
- Cherry tomatoes
- Cucumbers
- Daikon
- Fennel
- Jícama
- Mushrooms
- Radishes
- Scallions
- Sugar snap peas
- Zucchini and other summer squash

vegetables best eaten when blanched

- Asparagus
- Broccoli; broccolini
- Cauliflower
- Green beans
- Snow peas

how to stock a party pantry

If you are prepared, dips and spreads are the perfect solution to entertaining unexpected guests. Stock your freezer with pita bread, baguettes, bagels, tortillas, won ton wrappers, and basil pesto. Try to keep at least a small container of sour cream and a package of cream cheese on hand in the refrigerator, plus a few interesting cheeses, including Parmesan. Garlic is a pantry essential, and fresh ginger and herbs are always a plus. Here is a list of convenient pantry foods for easy entertaining:

- Anchovies packed in olive oil
- Canned artichoke hearts
- Balsamic vinegar
- Canned beans—black, white, and garbanzo
- Capers
- Chili paste—either Chinese chili paste with garlic or Indonesian *sambal oelek*
- Canned unsweetened coconut milk
- Crackers and bread sticks, assorted
- Dijon mustard
- Extra virgin olive oil
- Asian fish sauce—*nuoc nam* or *nam pla*
- Herbs and spices, assorted, including smoked paprika
- Horseradish
- Hot sauce, such as Tabasco
- Lemons and/or limes
- Mayonnaise
- Nuts—almonds, walnuts, pine nuts, etc.
- Olives—as many varieties as possible
- Peanut butter
- Pomegranate molasses
- Poppadums

- Potato chips
- Roasted red peppers and/or piquillo peppers, canned or bottled
- Sesame oil, Asian
- Soy sauce
- Sun-dried tomatoes
- Tahini (sesame seed paste)
- Tortilla chips

a note about the recipes

While proportions can be critical with many recipes, especially baking recipes, these dips and spreads can all be multiplied exactly to accommodate larger parties.

cool
dips
and
spreads

cannellini bean dip with crispy pancetta and
   fresh thyme 20

artichoke-asiago dip with lemon 22

babaganoush with pomegranate molasses 23

shanghai eggplant dip 24

garlicky orange-basil dip 25

greek cucumber-yogurt dip 27

creamy herb dip 28

guacamole with jalapeño and lime 29

creamy horseradish dipping sauce with fresh chives 30

caramelized onion dip 31

hummus with smoked paprika 32

spicy peanut dipping sauce 34

southeast asian dipping sauce with carrots
  and chiles 35

romesco sauce 37

fresh spinach dip with feta and dill 38

sun-dried tomato aioli 41

wild mushroom and walnut pâté 42

chunky blue cheese dip 43

brie with pesto and pine nuts 45

cocktail cheese spread 46

chicken liver pâté with marsala and capers 47

creamy crab dip 48

bay shrimp with cream cheese and cilantro
  cocktail sauce 51

smoked salmon spread with scotch whisky 52

fresh tuna pâté with pistachios 55

24-carat caviar dip 56

potted shrimp with lemon and fresh nutmeg 58

creamy chile and olive dip 59

three-berry yogurt dip 61

chocolate velvet dip 62

tropical ginger-lime dipping sauce 64

luscious lemon dip 65

peanut butter marshmallow dip 66

pumpkin cheesecake dip 67

cannellini bean dip
with crispy pancetta and fresh thyme

Like all beans, kidney-shaped white Italian cannellini beans are low in fat and high in fiber. Best of all, they taste rich and meaty, which makes them the perfect base for this satisfying dip. Pancetta, Italian unsmoked bacon, is available at many supermarket deli sections and at Italian food shops. Since it is used diced, purchase chopped pancetta or buy a chunk rather than thin slices.

▶ *Makes about 2 cups; serves 10 to 12*

---

3 tablespoons extra-virgin olive oil

4 ounces pancetta, finely diced

½ cup finely chopped onion

1 tablespoon chopped fresh thyme or 1 teaspoon dried thyme leaves

¼ teaspoon crushed hot red pepper

1 garlic clove, minced

2 cans (19 ounces each) cannellini or other white beans, rinsed and well drained

¼ cup chicken broth

1 In a large saucepan, heat 1 tablespoon of the olive oil over medium heat. Add the pancetta and cook, stirring frequently, until lightly browned and crisp, 3 to 5 minutes. Stir in the onion, thyme, and hot pepper. Cook, stirring occasionally, until the onion is softened but not browned, about 3 minutes. Add the garlic and cook for 1 minute longer.

2 Add the cannellini beans and cook for 2 minutes, coarsely mashing the beans with a fork. Stir in the remaining 2 tablespoons olive oil and the chicken broth and cook for 1 minute. Remove from the heat and let cool to room temperature.

3 Transfer to a bowl and serve at once, or cover and refrigerate for up to 3 days. Let return to room temperature and stir again before serving.

artichoke-asiago
dip with lemon

Canned artichoke hearts add body and texture to this party dip, which pairs the vegetable with two popular Italian cheeses: rich, creamy mascarpone and Asiago, a sharp, Parmesan-like cheese. Serve with crisp raw vegetables and bread sticks for dipping, or spread on whole-grain crackers or Crostini (page 119).

▶ *Makes about 2 cups; serves 8 to 10*

¼ cup loosely packed flat-leaf parsley

1 garlic clove, coarsely chopped

¼ teaspoon salt

8 ounces mascarpone cheese

2 tablespoons extra-virgin olive oil

Finely grated zest of 1 lemon

2 teaspoons fresh lemon juice

⅛ teaspoon hot pepper sauce, such as Tabasco

1 can (about 14 ounces) artichoke hearts, drained

½ cup freshly grated Asiago cheese

1 In a food processor, combine the parsley, garlic, and salt. Pulse until the parsley is coarsely chopped. Add the mascarpone, olive oil, lemon zest, lemon juice, and hot sauce. Pulse once or twice to blend. Add the drained artichokes and grated Asiago cheese and pulse just until the artichokes are finely chopped.

2 Transfer to a bowl and serve at once, or cover and refrigerate for up to 2 days. Let return to cool room temperature before serving.

babaganoush with pomegranate molasses

Pomegranate molasses, which is sold in Middle Eastern grocery stores and in the international section of many supermarkets, has a rich, fruity, sweet-tart taste. For extra color, add 2 tablespoons of chopped parsley to the finished dip and garnish, if you like, with fresh pomegranate seeds. Serve with Baked Pita Chips (page 124) or baby carrots.

▶ *Makes about 1¾ cups; serves 6 to 8*

---

1 large firm eggplant (1¼ to 1½ pounds)

3 tablespoons tahini (Middle Eastern sesame paste)

1 tablespoon pomegranate molasses

1 tablespoon lemon juice

1 tablespoon extra-virgin olive oil

1 garlic clove, crushed

½ teaspoon ground cumin

¼ teaspoon salt

¼ teaspoon Aleppo pepper or ⅛ teaspoon cayenne pepper

1 Preheat the oven to 450°F. Prick the eggplant in several places with the tip of a knife. Roast the eggplant in a shallow baking pan, turning once, until the outside is blackened and wrinkled and the eggplant is partially deflated, 50 to 60 minutes. Remove to a colander and let cool.

2 Cut the eggplant open, letting any juices run off. Scrape the eggplant off the skin and discard the skin. In a food processor, pulse the eggplant with the tahini 6 to 8 times to chop the eggplant and mix the two together. Scrape into a bowl. Add the pomegranate molasses, lemon juice, olive oil, garlic, cumin, salt, and Aleppo pepper. Mix well.

3 Transfer the babaganoush to a bowl and serve at once or let stand at room temperature for up to 2 hours, or cover and refrigerate for up to 2 days.

shanghai eggplant dip

Asian flavors whipped up with roasted eggplant create a smooth and silky vegetarian dip that's savory and enticing. Serve with Won Ton Crisps (page 121), Baked Pita Chips (page 124), or assorted fresh vegetables.

▶ *Makes about 2¼ cups; serves 10 to 12*

---

2 large eggplants, about 1½ pounds each

3 garlic cloves, coarsely chopped

½ teaspoon salt

2 tablespoons soy sauce

2 tablespoons cider vinegar

4 teaspoons finely grated fresh ginger

4 teaspoons Asian sesame oil

1½ teaspoons Asian chili paste

2 tablespoons chopped cilantro or parsley

1 Preheat the oven to 450°F. Prick the eggplants in several places with the tip of a knife. Roast in a shallow baking pan, turning once, until the skins are blackened and wrinkled and the eggplants are partially deflated, 50 to 60 minutes. Remove to a colander and let cool.

2 Cut the eggplants open, letting any juices run off. Scrape the eggplant off the skin and discard the skin. In a food processor, combine the garlic and salt. Pulse until finely chopped. Add the eggplant, soy sauce, vinegar, ginger, sesame oil, and chili paste. Puree until smooth. Season with additional salt to taste, if needed.

3 Scrape the dip into a small serving bowl and stir in 1½ tablespoons of the cilantro. Sprinkle the remaining cilantro over the top. Serve at once, or cover and refrigerate for up to 24 hours.

garlicky
orange-basil dip

Frozen orange juice concentrate and Grand Marnier are the secret ingredients that lend a hint of orange to this pungent dip. It's perfect with a basket of crudités, grilled or chilled shrimp, cocktail-size crab cakes, or skewered scallops.

► *Makes about 1¾ cups; serves 8 to 10*

1½ cups mayonnaise

4 teaspoons frozen orange juice concentrate, thawed

1 tablespoon Grand Marnier, Triple Sec, or other orange-flavored liqueur

1½ teaspoons Dijon mustard

2½ tablespoons finely chopped fresh basil

1 tablespoon grated orange zest

1½ teaspoons minced shallot

⅛ teaspoon cayenne pepper

Dash of salt

1 In a medium bowl, whisk together the mayonnaise, orange juice concentrate, Grand Marnier, and mustard until well blended. Stir in the basil, orange zest, shallot, cayenne, and salt.

2 Transfer the dip to a small bowl. Cover and refrigerate for at least 2 hours or up to 2 days before serving to allow the flavors to mellow.

greek cucumber-yogurt dip

Thickened yogurt makes all the difference in this traditional creamy tzatziki. While many stores stock Greek-style yogurt, I recommend draining regular plain yogurt overnight to ensure proper texture, so be sure to plan ahead. Serve with wedges of fresh pita bread or Baked Pita Chips (page 124) and assorted fresh vegetables.

▶ *Makes about 3 cups; serves 10 to 12*

---

2 cups plain yogurt

1 English hothouse cucumber, halved lengthwise, seeded, and coarsely grated

1 tablespoon coarse kosher salt

½ cup sour cream

2 tablespoons fresh lemon juice

1½ tablespoons finely chopped fresh dill

2 teaspoons finely chopped fresh mint

1 garlic clove, crushed through a press

¼ teaspoon ground cumin

Freshly ground black pepper

1 Line a sieve with cheesecloth, an unbleached coffee filter, or a double layer of white paper towels and place over a medium bowl. Spoon the yogurt into the lined sieve, cover with plastic wrap, and let drain in the refrigerator overnight.

2 In another bowl, toss the cucumber with the salt. Cover and refrigerate for 3 hours.

3 Transfer the drained yogurt to a clean bowl. (Discard the liquid, or whey, or save for soup stock.) Stir in the sour cream, lemon juice, dill, mint, garlic, and cumin. With your hands, squeeze out as much liquid as possible from the cucumber. Add the cucumber to the herbed yogurt mixture and stir to mix. Season with pepper to taste.

4 Transfer the dip to a bowl and cover and refrigerate for at least 2 or up to 8 hours before serving to allow the flavors to develop.

creamy herb dip

An easy garden-fresh dip is always a welcome accompaniment to a basket of crunchy crudités. Potato chips, Won Ton Crisps (page 121), or Poppadums (page 122) also go well. For variation, substitute chopped fresh tarragon or basil for the dill.

► *Makes about 1 ⅔ cups; serves 8 to 10*

¾ cup sour cream

¾ cup mayonnaise

3 tablespoons finely chopped parsley

3 tablespoons minced fresh chives

3 tablespoons finely chopped fresh dill

1 teaspoon fresh lemon juice

¼ teaspoon salt

Dash of cayenne pepper

1 In a small bowl, combine the sour cream, mayonnaise, parsley, chives, dill, lemon juice, salt, and cayenne. Stir until well mixed.

2 Transfer to a small bowl and serve at once, or cover and refrigerate for up to 8 hours.

guacamole
with jalapeño and lime

Rinsing peeled avocado in a bowl of water as directed here may sound odd, but it really helps maintain the fresh green color, even after mashing. Serve this zesty guacamole with tortilla chips and assorted fresh vegetables like jícama and celery sticks, red bell pepper strips, and cauliflower florets.

▶ *Makes about 3 cups; serves 10 to 12*

---

3 ripe avocados

2 tablespoons fresh lime juice

1 small tomato, seeded and chopped

⅓ cup finely chopped white or red onion

1 fresh jalapeño pepper, seeded and finely chopped

Salt

1 Cut the avocados in half lengthwise and discard the pits. Using a large spoon, or avocado peeler, scoop the avocado from the skins and rinse quickly in a bowl of cold water to prevent darkening. Drain well.

2 In a medium bowl, use an old-fashioned potato masher or the tines of a fork to mash the avocados, leaving some texture. Mix in the lime juice, then stir in the tomato, onion, and jalapeño. Season with salt to taste.

3 Transfer to a small bowl and serve at once or cover with plastic wrap directly touching the surface and refrigerate for up to 3 hours.

creamy horseradish dipping sauce with fresh chives

Whipped cream adds lightness to this herb-flecked sauce, the perfect accompaniment to appetizer-size beef or lamb kebabs or chunks of smoked trout. It also works extremely well as a dip for vegetables and prawns or shrimp.

▶ *Makes 1¼ cups; serves 6 to 8*

½ cup sour cream

¼ cup mayonnaise

2 teaspoons honey-Dijon mustard

2 tablespoons prepared white horseradish, or more to taste

¼ teaspoon ground white pepper

½ cup heavy cream

1 tablespoon minced fresh chives

1 In a medium bowl, combine the sour cream, mayonnaise, mustard, horseradish, and white pepper.

2 In another bowl, whip the cream until it forms stiff peaks. Fold the whipped cream and chives into the horseradish mixture until blended.

3 Transfer to a small bowl, cover, and refrigerate for at least 2 hours or up to 3 days before serving.

caramelized
onion dip

Making the granddaddy of all dips need not begin with an envelope of salty dried soup mix. Here's a luscious, sophisticated version of the classic that takes its cue from French onion soup, cooking real onions with a hint of balsamic vinegar until they are golden brown and meltingly tender. Serve with potato chips, of course, or Baked Pita Chips (page 124) and crisp vegetables.

▶ *Makes about 2 cups; serves 8*

2 tablespoons extra-virgin olive oil

2 large onions, quartered lengthwise and thinly sliced

1 teaspoon balsamic vinegar

½ teaspoon salt

¼ teaspoon freshly ground black pepper

1 cup sour cream

4 ounces cream cheese, at room temperature

1 In a large heavy skillet, warm the olive oil over medium-low heat. Stir in the onions, balsamic vinegar, salt, and pepper. Cover the skillet and cook for 5 minutes. Uncover, raise the heat to medium, and continue to cook, stirring occasionally, until the onions are soft and golden brown, 35 to 40 minutes. Remove from the heat and let cool.

2 In a medium bowl, combine the sour cream and cream cheese. Beat until smooth and well blended. Stir in the browned onions with all their oil and juices.

3 Transfer to a serving bowl, cover, and refrigerate for at least 4 hours or up to 2 days. Before serving, stir again and let stand at room temperature for 15 minutes.

hummus with smoked paprika

Hummus is a five-minute dip you can whip up on the spur of the moment. While it lends itself to many flavors, the smokiness of paprika and chipotle make this version distinctive. The peppers also add a nice blush to the color. When serving, garnish with a dusting of smoked paprika and a drizzle of olive oil, if you like.

► *Makes 2½ cups; serves 8 to 12*

---

1 can (15.5 ounces) chickpeas (garbanzo beans), rinsed and well drained

¼ cup tahini (Middle Eastern sesame paste), preferably the soft jarred variety

¼ cup fruity extra-virgin olive oil

3 tablespoons fresh lemon juice

1 garlic clove, smashed and chopped

1 teaspoon smoked paprika, preferably bittersweet

½ teaspoon ground cumin

½ teaspoon salt

Dash of chipotle chile powder

1 In a food processor, combine the chickpeas, tahini, olive oil, lemon juice, and garlic. Blend briefly. With the machine on, add ½ cup of warm water and puree until smooth. Add the smoked paprika, cumin, salt, and chipotle powder. Process until thoroughly blended.

2 Transfer the dip to a colorful dish and serve at once, or cover and refrigerate for up to 5 days.

spicy peanut
dipping sauce

Southeast Asian peanut sauce is a complex balance of salty, sweet, sour, and spicy, achieved using only a few ingredients. Serve this irresistible dip with celery sticks and other crisp vegetables, beef or chicken satays, apple wedges, or Won Ton Crisps (page 121).

▶ *Makes about 1¼ cups; serves 6 to 8*

⅔ cup smooth peanut butter (not natural-style)

⅔ cup well-shaken canned unsweetened coconut milk

2½ teaspoons Asian fish sauce (see Note) or soy sauce

2 tablespoons fresh lime juice

2 tablespoons light brown sugar

1½ teaspoons Asian chili paste

1 In a medium bowl, combine the peanut butter, coconut milk, fish sauce, lime juice, brown sugar, and chili paste. Stir to blend well.

2 Transfer to a small bowl and serve at once, or cover and refrigerate for up to 3 days. Let return to room temperature and stir again before serving.

NOTE: Fish sauce is known as *nuoc nam* in Vietnam and *nam pla* in Thailand. It is available in Asian grocery stores and in the Asian foods section of most supermarkets.

southeast asian dipping sauce with carrots and chiles

Use this light and lively Thai-inspired sauce for dipping large shrimp, seafood kebabs, or any spring rolls or other Chinese dumplings.

▶ *Makes about ³/₄ cup; serves 8 to 10*

---

3 garlic cloves, chopped

2 serrano or other small hot chile peppers, chopped (seeds and all)

3 tablespoons fresh lime juice

1½ tablespoons sugar

¼ cup Asian fish sauce (see Note on page 34)

1 small carrot, peeled and grated

1 In a small bowl, combine the garlic, chile peppers, lime juice, sugar, and fish sauce with ⅓ cup of water. Let stand at room temperature for 10 to 15 minutes.

2 Strain the sauce through a fine sieve into a bowl; discard the solids. Stir in the carrot.

3 Transfer to a bowl and serve at once, or cover and refrigerate for up to 8 hours.

romesco sauce

Spanish piquillo peppers are sold in jars and cans; they have a lovely fruity flavor, with just a hint of heat. Roasted red peppers can be substituted, but the flavor will not be the same. Note: While the sauce is offered as a dip here, a dollop goes beautifully with roast lamb or grilled salmon.

▶ *Makes about 1½ cups; serves 6 to 8*

½ cup whole natural almonds

1 large plum tomato, halved lengthwise

3 large garlic cloves

½ teaspoon cumin seeds

4 ounces sliced drained piquillo peppers (a heaping ½ cup)

⅓ cup extra-virgin olive oil, preferably a Spanish variety

3 to 4 tablespoons fresh lemon juice

1 teaspoon smoked Spanish paprika (*pimentón de la Vera*), preferably bittersweet

⅛ teaspoon chipotle chile powder, or more to taste

½ teaspoon salt

1 Preheat the oven to 375°F. Spread out the almonds on a small baking sheet. Gently squeeze the tomato to remove most of the seeds and set cut sides down on the sheet. Add 2 of the garlic cloves in their skins. Toast for about 10 minutes, turning the garlic and stirring the nuts once, until the almonds are very lightly browned when broken open. Place the nuts in a blender or food processor. Peel the roasted garlic and add it along with the tomato halves.

2 In a small dry skillet, toast the cumin seeds over medium heat, shaking the pan from time to time, until they darken slightly and smell fragrant, about 2 minutes. Add to the blender. Mince the remaining garlic clove and add that as well. Add the piquillo peppers, olive oil, 3 tablespoons of the lemon juice, the smoked paprika, chipotle chile powder, salt, and ¼ cup of water. Pulse several times, then puree for 1 to 2 minutes until the sauce is smooth. Add 1 more tablespoon of lemon juice if you think it's needed. If the dip thickens upon standing, thin with a little more water.

3 Transfer the Romesco sauce to a bowl and serve at once, or cover and refrigerate for up to 3 days.

fresh spinach dip
with feta and dill

This emerald-colored spread is thick enough for Crostini (page 119), yet light enough to serve with Baked Pita Chips (page 124) and endive leaves, jícama sticks, and other fresh vegetables for dunking.

▶ *Makes about 1³/₄ cups; serves 8 to 10*

6 cups loosely packed fresh baby spinach leaves (about 5 ounces)

1 garlic clove, chopped

⅛ teaspoon salt

¾ cup ricotta cheese

1 cup crumbled feta cheese (4 ounces)

¼ cup extra-virgin olive oil

1 tablespoon fresh lemon juice

1 tablespoon chopped fresh dill or ½ teaspoon dried

Dash of cayenne pepper

1 Rinse the spinach in a large bowl of cold water. Drain but do not spin dry. Place the spinach with any water that still clings to the leaves in a large heavy nonreactive saucepan. Cover and cook over medium heat, turning over with tongs once or twice for even cooking, until the spinach is bright green and just wilted, 2 to 3 minutes. Transfer to a colander to drain. When cool enough to handle, squeeze dry with your hands.

2 In a food processor, combine the garlic and salt. Process until the garlic is finely chopped. Add the ricotta and puree until smooth, scraping down the sides of the bowl once or twice. Add the spinach, feta cheese, olive oil, lemon juice, dill, and cayenne. Pulse until the spinach is coarsely chopped and the cheese is blended.

3 Transfer to a bowl, cover with plastic wrap, and refrigerate for at least 1 hour or up to 6 hours before serving.

sun-dried
tomato aioli

Serve this colorful garlicky mayonnaise with assorted raw vegetables or tiny roasted new potatoes. The flavor is intense—in a good way—so only a dab is needed for each serving.

▶ *Makes about 1½ cups; serves 8 to 10*

---

20 oil-packed sun-dried tomato halves (about 1 cup), drained (about 4 ounces)

3 garlic cloves

¾ cup mayonnaise

2 teaspoons fresh lemon juice

½ teaspoon salt

⅛ teaspoon cayenne pepper

¼ cup extra-virgin olive oil

1 Combine the sun-dried tomatoes and garlic cloves in a food processor or blender. Pulse until finely chopped. Add the mayonnaise, lemon juice, salt, and cayenne. Process until well blended.

2 With the machine on, gradually add the olive oil in a thin stream until completely incorporated.

3 Transfer the aioli to a bowl and serve at once, or cover and refrigerate for up to 3 days.

wild mushroom
and walnut pâté

A mix of wild mushrooms contributes incomparable woodsy flavor, but the recipe can be made simply with a pound of cremini, Italian brown mushrooms. While the pâté can be served simply from a crock, it looks more impressive unmolded from a small loaf pan. Serve on a bed of ruffly green leaf lettuce or kale, garnished with sprigs of fresh thyme or parsley and accompanied by crisp celery sticks and baguette slices, crackers, bread sticks, or Crostini (page 119).

▶ *Makes about 2 ¼ cups; serves 8 to 10*

½ cup coarsely chopped walnuts

4 tablespoons unsalted butter, cut into 4 pieces

12 ounces assorted wild mushrooms, such as shiitake, chanterelle, morel, and oyster, trimmed and coarsely chopped

4 ounces cremini mushrooms, coarsely chopped

¼ cup chopped shallots

1½ teaspoons finely chopped fresh thyme or ½ teaspoon dried thyme leaves

½ teaspoon salt

2 tablespoons cognac or brandy

1 teaspoon soy sauce

4 ounces cream cheese, cut into 4 pieces, at room temperature

1 Preheat the oven to 325°F. Spread out the walnuts in a small baking pan and toast in the oven until lightly browned and fragrant, 8 to 10 minutes.

2 In a large skillet, melt the butter over medium heat. Add the wild mushrooms, cremini mushrooms, shallots, thyme, and salt. Increase the heat to medium-high and cook, stirring occasionally, until the shallots have softened and the mushroom liquid has almost all evaporated, about 7 minutes. Stir in the cognac and soy sauce and cook for 1 minute longer. Set aside for about 10 minutes to cool slightly.

3 In a food processor, combine the toasted walnuts and sautéed mushrooms. Pulse until finely chopped. Add the cream cheese and pulse until the pâté is evenly blended but still has some texture. Line a 2- to 2½-cup loaf pan, bowl, or other mold with plastic wrap. Pack the mushroom pâté inside, cover, and refrigerate for at least 4 hours or up to 2 days.

4 Invert the chilled pâté onto a serving plate to unmold, then peel off the plastic wrap. Alternatively, simply pack the mixture into a small crock or serving bowl. Serve at cool room temperature.

chunky blue cheese dip

Blue cheese dip is one of the easiest and most popular appetizers you can serve. Because it contains so few ingredients, the flavor is dependent on the quality of the cheese used. Choose a good American artisanal blue or a quality import, such as Point Reyes, Roquefort, or Bleu d'Auvergne. Accompany with a platter of assorted crudités or serve with celery sticks and Buffalo chicken wings.

▶ *Makes about 1³/₄ cups; serves 6 to 8*

---

1 cup sour cream

4 ounces blue cheese, coarsely crumbled

1½ tablespoons red wine vinegar

¼ teaspoon salt

Dash of cayenne pepper

1 In a small bowl, combine the sour cream, blue cheese, vinegar, salt, and cayenne. Stir to mix with a fork, mashing the cheese as you work.

2 Transfer to an attractive bowl and serve at once, or cover and refrigerate for up to 3 days.

brie with pesto and pine nuts

Simple but sophisticated, this three-ingredient appetizer is a guaranteed party pleaser. If you use a commercial pesto, drain off any excess oil before spreading it on the cheese. Crackers or sliced baguettes are all that is needed for serving.

▶ *Serves 8 to 10*

---

1 large wedge of Brie (about 12 ounces), well chilled

2 tablespoons basil pesto

1 tablespoon pine nuts (pignoli)

1 Spray the blade of a long, thin knife with no-stick cooking spray. Carefully cut the cheese in half horizontally. (If the cheese is too soft, freeze just until firm enough to slice; do not leave in the freezer, or the texture will be compromised.) Spread an even layer of pesto over the bottom half of the cheese to within ⅛ inch of the edge. (Resist the urge to use more pesto; too much filling will look messy.) Set the top of the Brie in place and press gently to sandwich the layers.

2 In a small dry skillet, toast the pine nuts over medium-low heat, shaking the pan frequently, until lightly browned and fragrant, 2 to 3 minutes. Immediately scatter the warm pine nuts over the rind of the cheese, pressing them in gently.

3 Set the cheese aside at room temperature for up to 3 hours before serving.

NOTE: For large parties of 20 or more, purchase a 1-kilo wheel of Brie (about 2 pounds) and fill it with ½ cup of pesto. Top with about 3 tablespoons of pine nuts.

cocktail cheese spread

Here's something to do with all those bits of cheese that seem to accumulate in the back of the refrigerator. The French call this *fromage fort*; some dubious American renditions are known simply as "bar cheese." Serve with baguette slices, peppery crackers, Crostini (page 119), or crisp celery sticks and radishes.

▶ *Makes about 1¼ cups; serves 4 to 6*

---

8 ounces assorted cheeses, such as cheddar, Brie, and Parmesan, at room temperature

¼ cup dry white wine or dry vermouth

1 tablespoon unsalted butter, at room temperature

1 tablespoon chopped fresh rosemary, tarragon, or thyme, or ½ teaspoon dried

1 garlic clove, finely minced

Coarsely cracked black pepper

1 Cut off and discard any rinds from the cheeses. Cut the soft cheeses into ½-inch cubes. Shred or finely chop the hard cheeses.

2 In a food processor, combine the cheeses, wine, butter, rosemary, garlic, and pepper to taste. Process, scraping down the sides of the bowl as needed, until the mixture is smooth and well blended, 30 seconds to 1 minute.

3 Transfer the cheese spread to a small crock or ramekin and serve at once or cover and refrigerate for up to 4 days.

chicken liver pâté
with marsala and capers

This Italian treatment is a little unusual and very delicious. Anchovy paste is the potent secret ingredient here, but if you don't tell, no one will guess it's there. Serve with crackers, bread rounds, or Crostini (page 119).

▶ *Makes about 1½ cups; serves 8*

1 pound chicken livers

2 tablespoons unsalted butter, cut into pieces

2 tablespoons extra-virgin olive oil

¼ cup finely chopped onion

⅓ cup dry Marsala or sherry

2½ tablespoons anchovy paste

1 jar (3 ounces) capers, drained

Freshly ground black pepper

1 Pat the chicken livers dry and trim off any thick veins and yellow or green bits. Divide into lobes.

2 In a large skillet, melt the butter in the olive oil over medium heat. Add the onion and cook, stirring, to soften slightly, 1 to 2 minutes. Raise the heat to medium-high and add the chicken livers. Sauté, tossing occasionally, until they are browned outside but still slightly pink in the center, about 3 minutes. Use a slotted spoon to remove the livers to a bowl.

3 Pour the Marsala into the skillet and boil until all but 1 tablespoon has evaporated. Scrape the liquid from the skillet over the livers. Let cool for 5 to 10 minutes. Using the tines of a fork, mix in the anchovy paste and then the capers, coarsely mashing the chicken livers in the process. Season generously with pepper to taste.

4 Transfer to a small crock or serving bowl and cover with plastic wrap. Refrigerate for at least 30 minutes or as long as 2 days to allow the flavors to develop. Serve slightly chilled.

creamy crab dip

Almost everyone loves crab, and while it is pricey, it requires no cooking or preparation—plus a little goes a long way. Dotted with bits of sweet red pepper, this dip is especially attractive, and it's easily assembled from many items you probably already have in your pantry. Serve with water biscuits, toasted brioche, or endive spears.

▶ *Makes about 1³/₄ cups; serves 6 to 8*

---

8 ounces cream cheese, at room temperature

¹/₃ cup mayonnaise

1 teaspoon fresh lemon juice

1 teaspoon prepared white horseradish

¹/₄ teaspoon celery salt

8 ounces lump crabmeat, picked over to remove any bits of shell or cartilage, and well drained

2 tablespoons finely chopped red bell pepper

1 scallion, finely chopped

1 In a medium bowl, combine the cream cheese, mayonnaise, lemon juice, horseradish, and celery salt. Mix until well blended.

2 Stir in the crab, bell pepper, and scallion.

3 Transfer to a small serving bowl, cover, and chill for 2 hours or overnight to allow the flavors to develop. Remove from the refrigerator about 15 minutes before serving.

bay shrimp with cream cheese and cilantro cocktail sauce

Bay shrimp, which are tiny and already cooked and peeled, are sold in cans, frozen, and loose in fish markets. Opt for fresh if you can find them. Serve this popular spread with crackers, small slices of dark rye bread, Crostini (page 119), or Rosemary Focaccia (page 120). Chili sauce is sold next to the ketchup in most supermarkets.

▶ *Serves 6 to 8*

---

8 ounces cream cheese

¾ cup bottled chili sauce

1 scallion, thinly sliced

1½ tablespoons chopped cilantro, plus a few sprigs for garnish

1 tablespoon fresh lemon juice

2 teaspoons prepared white horseradish

⅛ teaspoon hot pepper sauce, such as Tabasco

12 ounces (about 1½ cups) bay shrimp, rinsed if canned, well drained

1 Place the cream cheese in the center of a serving plate. Set aside at room temperature for about half an hour to soften.

2 Meanwhile, make the cocktail sauce: In a small bowl, combine the chili sauce, scallion, chopped cilantro, 2 teaspoons of the lemon juice, the horseradish, and hot sauce. Stir until well blended.

3 Spoon the sauce over the cream cheese, letting it drip down the sides and onto the plate. Mound the shrimp on top and drizzle the remaining 1 teaspoon lemon juice over them. Garnish with cilantro sprigs and serve at once.

smoked salmon spread with scotch whisky

Scotch may sound surprising in a dip, but the smokiness of the liquor pairs beautifully with the cured salmon and contributes an unexpected hit of flavor. Because the salmon is chopped here, you can save quite a bit by purchasing trimmings instead of perfect slices. Serve this marvelous spread with mini-bagels, cocktail rye or pumpernickel bread, or cucumber slices. To transform into a dip for vegetables or Bagel Chips (page 118), add 2 tablespoons of sour cream along with the cream cheese in step 1.

▶ *Makes about 2 cups; serves 8 to 10*

---

8 ounces cream cheese, at room temperature

2½ tablespoons Scotch whisky

1 tablespoon fresh lemon juice

½ teaspoon prepared white horseradish

8 ounces smoked salmon, chopped

2 scallions, thinly sliced

1 In a medium bowl, combine the cream cheese, Scotch, lemon juice, and horseradish. Beat until smooth. Stir in the smoked salmon and scallions.

2 Transfer to a small serving bowl, cover, and refrigerate for at least 1 hour or up to 2 days. Let stand at room temperature for 15 minutes before serving.

fresh tuna pâté
with pistachios

Fresh tuna has a very different taste than canned, and its dense texture makes a wonderful spread. Just be sure you don't overcook the fish, or the finished pâté will not be moist and creamy. Serve with crisp celery sticks and radishes; plain crackers, such as water biscuits; Crostini (page 119); or toasted cocktail rye.

▶ *Makes about 2¹/₂ cups; serves 10 to 12*

¼ cup dry white wine or vermouth

2 tablespoons coarsely chopped onion

8 ounces fresh tuna, cut about ¾ inch thick

8 ounces cream cheese, cut into pieces, at room temperature

¼ cup cognac or brandy

1¼ teaspoons coarsely cracked black pepper

½ teaspoon salt

2 hard-boiled eggs, coarsely chopped

¼ cup coarsely chopped fresh dill

7 tablespoons shelled pistachio nuts, coarsely chopped

1 In a nonreactive medium sauté pan or skillet, combine the wine and onion with enough water to reach halfway up the sides of the pan. Bring to a boil over medium-high heat. Add the tuna. Cover the pan and reduce the heat to low so the liquid is just simmering. Cook until the tuna is opaque on the outside and just barely pink in the center, 8 to 10 minutes. With a slotted spatula, transfer the tuna to a plate; cover with plastic wrap and refrigerate until cool, at least 2 hours or overnight.

2 Break up the tuna into a food processor. Add the cream cheese, cognac, pepper, and salt. Puree until smooth. Add the hard-boiled eggs and dill. Pulse until the mixture is well blended but still maintains some texture. Add 6 tablespoons of the pistachio nuts and pulse 2 or 3 times until mixed.

3 Scrape the pâté into a small crock or ramekin, cover, and refrigerate for at least 4 hours or up to 24 hours. Just before serving, garnish with the remaining 1 tablespoon chopped pistachios.

24-carat caviar dip

Golden whitefish caviar has a pleasingly crisp texture and mild flavor. Best of all, it is one of the least expensive caviars you can buy, and it looks great in a dip. Serve with potato chips or endive spears.

▶ *Makes about 1³/₄ cups; serves 6 to 8*

1¼ cups sour cream

2 ounces reduced-fat cream cheese (Neufchâtel), at room temperature

Dash of cayenne pepper

2 ounces golden white-fish caviar

¼ cup minced fresh chives

1 In a small bowl, combine the sour cream, cream cheese, and cayenne. Stir until completely blended. Add the caviar and chives and stir gently just until evenly mixed.

2 Serve at once, or cover and refrigerate for up to 2 days.

potted shrimp
with lemon and fresh nutmeg

This rich British spread is traditionally served with small triangles of thinly sliced toast. Since it is such an important element in this recipe, use a high-quality European-style butter whenever possible. It has a lower water content and creamier taste. Serve with crackers, cocktail pumpernickel bread, or small toasts.

▶ *Makes about 2 cups; serves 6 to 8*

1½ sticks (6 ounces) unsalted butter, cut into pieces

¾ teaspoon freshly grated nutmeg

½ teaspoon ground allspice

½ teaspoon salt

⅛ teaspoon ground white pepper

Dash of cayenne pepper

1 pound (about 2 cups) tiny shelled cooked shrimp, well drained

1 tablespoon fresh lemon juice

1 In a medium saucepan, melt the butter over low heat. Stir in the nutmeg, allspice, salt, white pepper, and cayenne. Add the shrimp, stir to coat, and cook for 3 minutes; do not let the butter brown. Remove from the heat and stir in the lemon juice.

2 Scrape the shrimp and spiced butter into a bowl. Cover and refrigerate until the butter begins to congeal, 15 to 20 minutes. Stir to mix, then pack the shrimp and butter into a 2-cup ramekin, crock, or other small serving bowl.

3 Cover and refrigerate for at least 4 hours, or until the spread is firm. The potted shrimp will keep well for up to 3 days. Let stand at room temperature for 30 minutes before serving to allow the spread to soften slightly.

creamy chile and olive dip

A cool, creamy base softens the zesty flavors traditionally found in many Mexican favorites. Serve this with scoop-shaped corn chips or tortilla chips.

► *Makes about 2¹/₂ cups; serves 8 to 10*

1 cup small-curd cottage cheese

1 cup mayonnaise

1 tomato, seeded and chopped

1 can (4.25 ounces) chopped ripe olives

1 can (4 ounces) diced mild green chiles

4 scallions, chopped

3 garlic cloves, crushed through a press

1 tablespoon chopped cilantro

1 In a medium bowl, combine the cottage cheese, mayonnaise, tomato, olives, green chiles, scallions, garlic, and cilantro. Stir until well blended.

2 Transfer to a bowl; cover and refrigerate for at least 2 hours or overnight before serving to allow the flavors to develop.

three-berry yogurt dip

Serve this cool dessert or snack dip with strawberries and other fresh fruit or with madeleines, brownie bites, shortbread cookies, small squares of angel food cake, or graham crackers.

▶ *Makes about 1 1/2 cups; serves 6*

⅔ cup frozen mixed berries, thawed

3 tablespoons confectioners' sugar

16 ounces plain yogurt, preferably Greek-style

1½ teaspoons Amaretto or ½ teaspoon almond extract

1 Puree the berries in a food processor or blender. Press through a sieve to remove the seeds, if you like.

2 In a medium bowl, combine the berry puree with the confectioners' sugar. Stir until the sugar dissolves. Whisk in the yogurt and Amaretto until well blended.

3 Serve at once, or cover and refrigerate for up to 24 hours. Whisk again before serving.

chocolate velvet dip

This lush dessert dip is remarkably rich and chocolaty. It makes an ideal embellishment for fresh strawberries, dried apricots, pretzels, butter cookies, macaroons, or cubes of pound cake.

▶ *Makes about 1 ½ cups; serves 6 to 8*

---

1 cup sour cream

½ cup unsweetened Dutch-process cocoa powder

½ cup honey

1 teaspoon vanilla extract

Dash of salt

1 In a medium bowl, combine the sour cream, cocoa powder, honey, vanilla, and salt. Whisk until smooth.

2 Transfer to a small serving bowl and serve at once, or cover and refrigerate for up to 3 days.

tropical ginger-lime dipping sauce

Fruit is the perfect vehicle to enjoy with this refreshing dip. Serve with whole strawberries, pineapple spears, apple wedges, and seedless grapes.

▶ *Makes about 1 ¼ cups; serves 4 to 6*

⅔ cup mayonnaise

⅓ cup sour cream

2 tablespoons honey

1 ½ teaspoons finely grated lime zest

2 tablespoons fresh lime juice

1 ½ teaspoons finely grated fresh ginger

1 In a small bowl, combine the mayonnaise, sour cream, honey, lime zest, lime juice, and ginger. Stir until well blended.

2 Transfer to a small bowl and serve at once, or cover and refrigerate for up to 3 days.

luscious lemon dip

Most supermarkets sell small jars of lemon curd, usually alongside the jams and jellies. It's a great product to keep on hand for all kinds of culinary emergencies, including this tart-sweet dip for crisp bite-size meringues, shortbread cookies, or fresh strawberries.

▶ *Makes about 1 cup; serves 4 to 6*

---

1 cup sour cream

¼ cup lemon curd

Grated zest of 1 lemon

2 teaspoons fresh lemon juice

1 In a small bowl, combine the sour cream, lemon curd, lemon zest, and lemon juice. Stir until well blended.

2 Transfer to an attractive small bowl and serve at once, or cover and refrigerate for up to 3 days.

peanut butter marshmallow dip

Many adults have fond memories of a childhood treat made from peanut butter and Marshmallow Fluff, usually sandwiched between two pieces of white bread. Adding a bit of sour cream to the mix balances the sweetness without losing the nostalgia—and makes a delicious dip suitable for kids of all ages. Serve with celery sticks, pretzels, graham crackers, chocolate wafers, apple wedges, banana chunks, or strawberries.

▶ *Makes about 1½ cups; serves 6 to 8*

---

1 cup peanut butter

1 cup Marshmallow Fluff or marshmallow crème

1 cup sour cream

1 In a medium bowl, combine the peanut butter, Marshmallow Fluff, and sour cream. Stir until well blended.

2 Transfer to a serving bowl and serve at once, or cover and refrigerate for up to 3 days. If needed, stir again before serving.

pumpkin cheesecake dip

If you're a fan of pumpkin, keep in mind that perfectly delicious canned pumpkin is available all year long. For added texture, add a handful of chopped candied pecans or minced candied ginger to this basic recipe. A tablespoon of dark rum would not be out of place, either. Serve with gingersnaps, graham crackers, biscotti, and apple wedges.

▶ *Makes about 2 cups; serves 8 to 10*

---

8 ounces cream cheese, at room temperature

⅓ cup packed dark brown sugar

2½ tablespoons unsulphured molasses

2 teaspoons pumpkin pie spice blend

⅛ teaspoon salt

1 cup canned unsweetened pure pumpkin puree

1 In a small bowl, combine the cream cheese, brown sugar, molasses, pumpkin pie spice, and salt. Mix until well blended. Add the pumpkin puree and stir until smooth.

2 Transfer to an attractive bowl and serve at once, or cover and refrigerate for up to 3 days. If chilled, let the dip stand at room temperature for at least 15 minutes before serving.

salsas and such

avocado salsa with tomatoes and scallions 70

fiery chipotle salsa 72

crunchy cucumber salsa with asian flavors 73

salsa fresca 75

tropical mango salsa 76

rockin' moroccan salsa 77

roasted corn salsa with poblano and lime 79

tomatillo salsa 80

italian cheese blend with hot pepper and sweet basil 81

plantation pineapple-chile salsa 82

garlicky italian salsa with peppers and olives 85

two-olive tapenade with capers 86

tamarind mint chutney 88

lemon-pistachio tuna tapenade 89

barbecued bean and bacon salsa 90

double pear salsa 91

avocado salsa
with tomatoes and scallions

Silky avocado makes a rich backdrop for this lively salsa, a chunky version of guacamole. Serve with fresh warm tortillas, corn or tortilla chips, or Baked Tortilla Chips (page 123).

► *Makes about 3 ½ cups; serves 10 to 12*

---

3 ripe avocados, preferably Hass variety

2 ripe medium tomatoes, seeded and chopped

½ cup thinly sliced scallions

½ cup coarsely chopped cilantro

¼ cup fresh lime juice

1 ½ teaspoons seeded and minced fresh jalapeño pepper

2 garlic cloves, finely minced

½ teaspoon salt

1 Cut the avocados in half lengthwise and discard the pits. Using a large spoon or avocado peeler, scoop out the flesh in a single piece, if possible. Cut the avocado into ⅜-inch dice and place in a bowl. Fill the bowl with cold water; lift out the avocado with a slotted spoon and drain on paper towels. (This will greatly reduce the amount of discoloration.)

2 In a medium bowl, combine the avocados, tomatoes, scallions, cilantro, lime juice, jalapeño, garlic, and salt. Toss gently to mix.

3 Transfer to a serving dish and serve at once, or cover with plastic wrap pressed directly onto the surface and refrigerate for up to 4 hours.

fiery chipotle salsa

Look for small cans of chipotle peppers in adobo in Latin markets and the Mexican food section of many supermarkets. Once opened, transfer the contents of the can to a small airtight jar; it will keep in the refrigerator for at least 6 months. This is a fairly smooth salsa that's good for dipping jícama or other vegetable sticks, grilled skewers of chicken or sausage, tortilla chips, or Baked Tortilla Chips (page 123).

► *Makes about 1¼ cups; serves 10 to 12*

---

2 tomatoes, coarsely chopped

1 small onion, coarsely chopped

4 canned chipotle chiles plus 3 tablespoons of adobo sauce from the can

¼ cup loosely packed fresh cilantro leaves

1 tablespoon fresh lime juice

2 teaspoons light brown sugar

¼ teaspoon salt

1 In a food processor or blender, combine the tomatoes, onion, chipotles with the 3 tablespoons adobo sauce, cilantro, lime juice, brown sugar, salt, and 1 tablespoon of water. Pulse until the mixture is very finely chopped but still maintains some texture.

2 Transfer the salsa to a small bowl and serve at once, or cover and refrigerate for up to 3 days.

crunchy cucumber salsa
with asian flavors

This uncooked salsa cruda relies on the same technique as Mexican salsa, but uses ingredients with a decidedly Asian cast. I leave the skin on the cucumber for color, but you can opt for peeling, if you prefer. Serve with Won Ton Crisps (page 121), Baked Pita Chips (124), or shrimp chips.

▶ *Makes about 2¼ cups; serves 6 to 8*

---

2 teaspoons hoisin sauce

2 teaspoons Asian sesame oil

1 teaspoon Asian chili paste, such as *sambal oelek*

2 cups seeded and finely diced English hot-house cucumber

4 scallions, thinly sliced

½ cup chopped cilantro

2 teaspoons finely grated fresh ginger

1 garlic clove, finely minced

1 In a medium bowl, combine the hoisin sauce, sesame oil, and chili paste. Stir to blend well. Add the cucumber, scallions, cilantro, ginger, and garlic. Toss gently to mix.

2 Transfer to a serving bowl and serve at once, or cover and refrigerate for up to 8 hours.

salsa fresca

While the name remains the same, fresh salsa is really a different food than jarred. Its flavors are bright and clear, its texture more defined. As long as you use the best vine-ripened tomatoes available, you are ensured success. Plum tomatoes have a higher ratio of flesh to seeds, so pick them whenever they are available.

▶ *Makes about 3 cups; serves 10 to 12*

1½ pounds vine-ripened tomatoes, seeded and cut into ⅜-inch dice

⅓ cup finely chopped white onion

¼ cup chopped cilantro

1 teaspoon seeded and finely chopped jalapeño pepper

3 tablespoons fresh lime juice

½ teaspoon salt

1 In a medium bowl, combine the tomatoes, onion, cilantro, jalapeño, lime juice, and salt. Toss gently to blend.

2 Transfer to a serving bowl, cover with plastic wrap, and let stand at room temperature for 30 minutes to allow the flavors to develop, or refrigerate for up to 8 hours. Return to room temperature before serving.

tropical mango salsa

Sweet and hot complement each other nicely, so it's no surprise that mangoes pair so naturally with hot chiles. This sunny salsa goes well with blue or yellow corn tortilla chips, Baked Tortilla Chips (page 123), as well as skewered grilled shrimp or chicken.

▶ *Makes about 2 cups; serves 6 to 8*

---

2 firm ripe mangoes, peeled, pitted, and cut into ½-inch dice

¼ cup chopped red onion

2 tablespoons chopped fresh mint or cilantro

1½ tablespoons fresh lime juice

½ teaspoon finely chopped fresh jalapeño pepper

Dash of salt

1 In a medium bowl, combine the mangoes, red onion, mint, lime juice, jalapeño, and salt. Toss gently to mix.

2 Transfer to a small bowl and serve at once, or cover and refrigerate for up to 4 hours.

rockin' moroccan salsa

This intriguing salsa takes its inspiration from *chermoula,* a traditional Moroccan accompaniment to seafood and vegetables. Serve with Baked Pita Chips (page 124), warm fresh pita bread, or Poppadums (page 122).

▶ *Makes about 1½ cups; serves 4 to 6*

---

2 medium tomatoes, chopped

⅓ cup chopped red onion

¼ cup chopped cilantro

1 tablespoon extra-virgin olive oil

2 teaspoons grated lemon zest

2 garlic cloves, minced

½ teaspoon ground cumin

¼ teaspoon ground cinnamon

¼ teaspoon ground turmeric

¼ teaspoon sweet paprika

⅛ teaspoon cayenne pepper

Dash of salt

1 In a small bowl, combine the tomatoes, red onion, cilantro, olive oil, lemon zest, garlic, cumin, cinnamon, turmeric, paprika, cayenne, and salt. Toss gently to mix.

2 Transfer to a serving bowl, cover, and let stand at room temperature for about 1 hour to allow the flavors to develop, or refrigerate for up to 8 hours. Serve at cool room temperature.

roasted corn salsa
with poblano and lime

Fresh corn is, of course, the first choice here, but thawed frozen organic corn kernels can be used with great success. Poblano chiles are usually fairly mild, but some mavericks can be surprisingly hot. To err on the safe side, taste the roasted peppers before adding the full amount to the salsa.

► *Makes about 2¾ cups; serves 10 to 12*

2 fresh poblano peppers

2 cups corn kernels (from about 4 ears of corn)

1 tablespoon olive oil

Salt and freshly ground black pepper

1 medium vine-ripened tomato, seeded and chopped

3 tablespoons finely chopped white onion

2 tablespoons fresh lime juice

¼ teaspoon salt

1 Place the peppers on a small baking sheet and broil as close to the heat as possible, turning with tongs, until charred all over, about 10 minutes. (Alternatively, roast the peppers directly over a gas flame, turning, until charred, about 5 minutes.) Seal the peppers in a paper bag and let steam for at least 10 minutes. Peel off the blackened skin. Cut the peppers open and discard the stems and seeds. Finely dice the poblanos.

2 Preheat the oven to 375°F. On a large baking sheet, toss the corn with the olive oil to coat. Season lightly with salt and pepper. Spread the corn out into an even layer and bake, stirring once or twice, until some of the kernels are lightly browned at the edges, about 10 minutes. Scrape into a medium bowl and let cool slightly.

3 Add the diced poblanos, tomato, onion, lime juice, and ¼ teaspoon salt. Toss gently to mix.

4 Transfer to a bowl and serve at once, or cover and refrigerate for up to 6 hours. Serve at room temperature or slightly chilled.

tomatillo salsa

Mexican *salsa verde* is made with tart tomatillos, which are usually available at Latin markets and many supermarkets. They resemble small green tomatoes with a thin, papery husk, which must be removed before using. Do not substitute canned in this recipe.

▶ *Makes about 1 1/2 cups; serves 4 to 6*

---

8 ounces fresh tomatillos, husked

1/3 cup finely chopped white onion

1/4 cup chopped cilantro

1 tablespoon fresh lime juice

1 fresh jalapeño pepper, seeded and minced

1 garlic clove, crushed through a press

1/2 teaspoon salt

1 In a medium saucepan of boiling water, cook the tomatillos over high heat for 1 minute. Drain in a colander and rinse under cold running water. Chop finely.

2 In a medium bowl, combine the tomatillos, onion, cilantro, lime juice, jalapeño, garlic, and salt.

3 Transfer to a bowl and serve at once, or cover and refrigerate for up to 8 hours. Serve at room temperature or slightly chilled.

italian cheese blend with hot pepper and sweet basil

Napa Valley Chef Michael Chiarello is known for his gutsy Italian food. This is my adaptation of his Salsa di Parmigiano—a condiment so popular he now sells it in jars. The blend of cheeses flavored with plenty of garlic, hot pepper, and fresh basil makes a memorable dip for endive leaves or broccoli florets, and a lusty spread for Crostini (page 119).

▶ *Makes about 1½ cups; serves 6 to 8*

3 garlic cloves, coarsely chopped

Dash of salt

8 ounces hard Italian cheeses, such as Parmigiano Reggiano, Asiago, Peppato, Grana Padano, and/or Pecorino Romano, broken into 1-inch chunks

1 teaspoon fresh lemon juice

½ teaspoon crushed hot red pepper

½ teaspoon coarsely cracked black pepper

¾ cup extra-virgin olive oil

¼ cup chopped fresh basil

1 Place the garlic in a food processor and sprinkle with a dash of salt. Pulse until the garlic is finely chopped. Add the cheeses, lemon juice, hot pepper, black pepper, and olive oil. Process for about 10 seconds, or until the cheese is broken into small bits. Scrape down the sides of the bowl with a rubber spatula. Add the basil and pulse once or twice more to blend.

2 Transfer to a bowl and serve. If not using within an hour or two, cover and refrigerate for up to 3 days. Let return to room temperature before serving.

plantation pineapple-chile salsa

Sweet pineapple, with its tropical overtones and acidic bite, makes a terrific salsa for shrimp, grilled sausage, Won Ton Crisps (page 121), or Baked Tortilla Chips (page 123).

▶ *Makes about 3 cups; serves 10 to 12*

½ ripe pineapple

½ cup chopped red bell pepper

⅓ cup coarsely chopped cilantro

¼ cup thinly sliced scallions

3 tablespoons fresh lime juice

1½ teaspoons finely chopped fresh jalapeño pepper

⅛ teaspoon salt

1 Trim the top and bottom from the pineapple half. Split in half lengthwise and remove the tough center core. Slice off the skin and remove the eyes. Cut the pineapple into ½-inch dice and place in a medium bowl. (There will be about 2½ cups.)

2 Add the bell pepper, cilantro, scallions, lime juice, jalapeño, and salt to the pineapple. Toss gently to mix.

3 Transfer to a small bowl and serve at once, or cover with plastic wrap and refrigerate for up to 4 hours.

garlicky italian salsa
with peppers and olives

When vine-ripened tomatoes are not in season, it's nice to consider other fruits and vegetables that chop up into beautiful, zesty salsas. Here sweet red peppers are the dominant ingredient, laced with the salty counterpoint of olives and capers. Serve with Crostini (page 119)—with or without a smear of soft cheese—for a delicious bruschetta.

▶ *Makes about 1 1/2 cups; serves 6 to 8*

3 large red bell peppers

1/3 cup chopped pitted oil-cured black olives (see Note)

2 1/2 tablespoons drained capers, coarsely chopped

2 1/2 tablespoons chopped parsley

3 tablespoons extra-virgin olive oil

2 teaspoons balsamic vinegar

1 garlic clove, finely minced

1/4 to 1/2 teaspoon crushed hot red pepper, to taste

Salt

1 Preheat the broiler, positioning the rack 4 to 6 inches from the heat. Place the peppers on a broiler pan and broil, turning frequently with tongs, until the skin is charred and blackened all over, about 10 minutes. (Alternatively, grill the peppers directly over a gas flame, turning, for about 5 minutes.) Seal the peppers in a brown paper bag and set aside to cool. Rub the skins off the peppers. Cut them open and discard the stems and seeds. Chop the peppers coarsely.

2 In a small bowl, combine the chopped roasted red peppers, olives, capers, parsley, olive oil, balsamic vinegar, garlic, and hot pepper. Toss gently to mix. Season with salt to taste.

3 Transfer the salsa to a small bowl. Cover and set aside for 1 hour at room temperature before serving to allow the flavors to develop, or refrigerate for up to 24 hours. If chilled, let stand for at least 15 minutes at room temperature before serving.

NOTE: Oil-cured olives are the drier, wrinkled kind that are not packed in brine. They are sold in bulk and in jars.

two-olive tapenade
with capers

Many commercial tapenades are processed into a smooth paste, which can muddy the bright olive flavor that should permeate this condiment. To ensure proper texture, forego the food processor and chop the olives by hand with a large sharp knife; it only takes a few minutes. This tapenade is especially nice spooned over a small log of goat cheese, to spread on Crostini (page 119) or crackers.

▶ *Makes about 1 cup; serves 4 to 6*

---

2 flat anchovy fillets packed in olive oil, drained

1 garlic clove, minced

½ cup drained picholine or other meaty green olives, pitted and finely chopped

½ cup drained pitted kalamata olives, finely chopped

¼ cup extra-virgin olive oil

2 tablespoons drained capers, coarsely chopped

1 teaspoon grated orange zest

1 teaspoon orange juice

1 teaspoon chopped fresh thyme or ¼ teaspoon dried thyme

Freshly ground black pepper

1 In a small bowl, combine the anchovies and garlic. Mash to a coarse paste with a fork. Add the picholine olives, kalamata olives, olive oil, capers, orange zest, orange juice, and thyme. Stir to mix well. Season with pepper to taste.

2 Transfer to a small crock or bowl and serve at once, or cover and refrigerate for up to 3 days.

tamarind mint chutney

Traditional Indian cuisine would make this into two recipes, sometimes stirred together into the same dish. Instead I combine the two
for an irresistible piquant dipping sauce that is excellent for fried
savory pastries, Won Ton Crisps (page 121), and skewered grilled
chicken or shrimp. Look for tamarind paste in Asian markets or the
Asian foods section of upscale supermarkets.

▶ *Makes about ¾ cup; serves 6*

---

1 tablespoon tamarind
paste

½ cup packed fresh
mint leaves

½ cup packed cilantro
leaves

1 teaspoon minced
fresh serrano chile or
¼ teaspoon crushed hot
red pepper

1 tablespoon minced
fresh ginger

1 teaspoon minced
garlic

1 tablespoon turbinado
("raw") or brown sugar

1 teaspoon salt

1 In a small bowl, dissolve the tamarind
paste in ½ cup warm water, stirring
until well blended. Scrape the tamarind
sauce into a food processor.

2 Add the mint, cilantro, chile pepper,
ginger, garlic, sugar, and salt. Puree
until the herbs are finely chopped.

3 Transfer to a bowl and serve.

lemon-pistachio
tuna tapenade

For a cocktail party spread or canapé topping, you'll find this bright-tasting tapenade easy and quick. To toast shelled pistachios, spread them out on a baking sheet and place in a 325°F oven for 5 to 7 minutes. Let cool slightly before using. Serve with crackers, small toasts, or thin rounds of raw zucchini or carrot cut at an angle to make them larger. Use a good-quality, fruity extra-virgin olive oil.

▶ *Makes 1¹/₂ cups; serves 6*

---

1 can (6 ounces) tuna packed in oil, drained

Zest and juice from 1 lemon, preferably organic

¹/₄ cup extra-virgin olive oil

1 scallion, finely chopped

1 garlic clove, minced

¹/₄ cup pimiento-stuffed Spanish olives

¹/₄ cup toasted pistachio nuts

Salt and freshly ground black pepper

1 Place the tuna, lemon zest and juice, olive oil, scallion, and garlic in a food processor and blend to a coarse puree. Add the olives and pistachios, and pulse 8 to 10 times to chop and mix into the tuna. Be sure to leave some bits of texture.

2 Turn into a small bowl and season with salt and pepper to taste. If not serving within the hour, cover and refrigerate for up to 2 days.

barbecued bean and bacon salsa

Why does three cups of zesty salsa serve only four to six people? Because everyone will want to eat it with a spoon. But the best way to serve this chunky dip is with corn chips and a generous supply of beer or tequila on the side.

► *Makes about 3 cups; serves 4 to 6*

---

5 strips of bacon

1 can (16 ounces) pinto beans

¼ cup finely chopped onion

1 tablespoon cider vinegar

¼ teaspoon salt

⅓ cup ketchup

1½ tablespoons olive oil or other vegetable oil

1 tablespoon dark brown sugar

1 teaspoon ground cumin

1 teaspoon chili powder

½ cup finely diced green bell pepper

½ cup finely diced red bell pepper

1 tablespoon minced pickled jalapeño pepper

1 Cook the bacon on a griddle or in a skillet over medium heat, turning several times, until the strips are golden brown and crisp. Drain on paper towels. Finely chop the bacon.

2 Rinse the beans very well and dry thoroughly. With a mezzaluna or large sharp chef's knife, coarsely chop the beans, leaving some whole; do not mash.

3 In a medium bowl, combine the onion, vinegar, and salt; stir to mix well. Add the ketchup, oil, brown sugar, cumin, and chili powder and blend well. Add the beans and stir gently to coat with sauce. Add the green and red bell peppers, jalapeños, and bacon. Toss to mix. Serve at room temperature.

double pear salsa

Dried pears add both a touch of sweetness and an unexpected textural element to this lively fruit salsa. It's a natural complement to cheeses served with Crostini (page 119) and assorted crackers. For the most striking color contrast, simply serve this salsa with a big bowl of blue corn tortilla chips.

▶ *Makes 2¹/₂ cups; serves 10 to 12*

---

2 firm but ripe pears, such as Bartlett or D'Anjou (about 1 pound)

2 dried pear halves, finely chopped

¹/₂ cup chopped red onion

¹/₄ cup chopped fresh mint

Juice and grated zest of 1 lime

1 jalapeño pepper, seeded and finely chopped

2 teaspoons finely grated fresh ginger

¹/₂ teaspoon salt

¹/₈ teaspoon crushed hot red pepper

1 Core the fresh pears and cut into ¹/₂-inch dice; no need to peel.

2 In a medium bowl, combine the cubed fresh pears, dried pears, red onion, mint, lime juice and zest, jalapeño, ginger, salt, and hot pepper. Toss gently to mix.

3 Transfer to a small serving bowl, cover, and refrigerate for at least 30 minutes to allow the flavors to develop. This salsa is best served the same day it is made.

warm
dips
and
spreads

warm artichoke dip with scallions and jalapeño 95
bagna cauda 96
california baked black bean dip 97
brie en croûte with apricot and almonds 98
baked brie with cranberry salsa 100
fiesta chili dip with ground turkey and corn 103
cowboy nacho dip 104
melted cheese with spicy chorizo 105
baked fontina with marinated mushrooms 106
baked fontina with artichokes 106
mexicali clam dip 107
goat cheese marinara with shredded basil 108
deviled shrimp with bacon 111
warm sweet and sour dip 112
warm olive pizza dip 113
chile con queso 114
crab amandine dip 115

warm artichoke dip with scallions and jalapeño

Many versions of this classic hot artichoke dip are way too oily for contemporary tastes. Substituting cream cheese for part of the mayonnaise corrects that problem and contributes extra body, which helps the dip hold together nicely. Serve with crisp raw vegetables, Baked Pita Chips (page 124), baguette slices, or crackers.

▶ *Makes about 2 cups; serves 8 to 10*

---

2 scallions, coarsely chopped

1½ teaspoons coarsely chopped pickled jalapeño pepper

1 garlic clove, cut into 2 or 3 pieces

Dash of salt

4 ounces cream cheese, cut into pieces, at room temperature

½ cup freshly grated Parmesan cheese

¼ cup mayonnaise

½ teaspoon fresh lemon juice

Dash of cayenne pepper

1 can (about 14 ounces) artichoke hearts, drained

1 Preheat the oven to 400°F.

2 In a food processor, combine the scallions, pickled jalapeño, garlic, and salt. Pulse until the scallions are finely chopped.

3 Add the cream cheese, all but 1 tablespoon of the Parmesan cheese, the mayonnaise, lemon juice, and cayenne. Puree until smooth. Add the artichokes and pulse until coarsely chopped.

4 Scrape the mixture into a 2-cup gratin or other shallow ovenproof baking dish. Sprinkle the reserved 1 tablespoon Parmesan cheese over the top. (At this point, the dip can be covered with plastic wrap and refrigerated for up to 24 hours before baking.)

5 Shortly before serving, bake for about 20 minutes, until the dip is lightly browned on top and bubbly hot. Let cool slightly before serving.

bagna cauda

Literally meaning "hot bath," this tantalizing appetizer from Italy is traditionally served with assorted vegetables—raw, blanched, or grilled. I also like to offer chunks of day-old Italian bread, bread sticks, or cooked shrimp. Serve in a ceramic fondue pot or chafing dish to keep it warm.

▶ *Makes about 2 cups; serves 8 to 10*

---

1 stick (4 ounces) unsalted butter, cut into pieces

1½ cups extra-virgin olive oil

1 can (2 ounces) flat anchovy fillets, chopped, oil reserved

8 large garlic cloves, minced

⅛ teaspoon salt

⅛ teaspoon crushed hot red pepper

1 tablespoon minced parsley

1 teaspoon fresh lemon juice

1 In a small saucepan, melt the butter in the olive oil over medium-low heat. Stir in the anchovies and their oil, the garlic, salt, and hot pepper. Cook, stirring to break up the anchovies, until the garlic is fragrant and the anchovies dissolve, 3 to 5 minutes.

2 Stir in the parsley and lemon juice.

3 Transfer to a fondue pot or chafing dish and serve at once. Regulate the heat under the pot, if possible, so the bagna cauda remains warm, not hot.

california baked
black bean dip

Canned refried beans are not known for their visual appeal, so for attractive presentation, this dip is dotted with shiny whole black beans and a tasty jumble of other ingredients that add both spice and color. Serve with corn chips, Baked Tortilla Chips (page 123), or assorted vegetables.

▶ *Makes about 3 1/2 cups; serves 12 to 16*

---

1 can (15 ounces) refried black beans

1 can (10 ounces) diced tomatoes with green chiles

1 1/2 cups (6 ounces) shredded Monterey Jack cheese

1/2 cup thinly sliced scallions

1/2 cup plus 1 table-spoon chopped cilantro

2 teaspoons ground cumin

1/2 teaspoon salt

1 can (15 ounces) black beans, rinsed and drained

1 Preheat the oven to 350°F.

2 In a medium bowl, combine the refried beans, tomatoes with chiles and all their juices, 1 cup of the cheese, the scallions, 1/2 cup of the cilantro, the cumin, and salt. Stir until well blended. Stir in the black beans.

3 Scrape the mixture into a 1-quart baking dish and top with the remaining 1/2 cup cheese. Bake for about 25 minutes, until the cheese has melted and the dip is bubbly hot.

4 Sprinkle the remaining 1 tablespoon cilantro on top and serve warm.

brie en croûte
with apricot and almonds

A loaf of bread makes a showy edible container for a small wheel of Brie. Two glistening layers of liqueur-infused fruit preserves sweeten the deal even further. Serve with small slices of the same bread used for the shell, and with crackers, crisp apple wedges, and dried apricots. When most of the cheese has been eaten, use a serrated knife to slice the loaf into serving-size pieces.

▶ *Serves 6 to 8*

---

1 small round loaf (8 ounces) French or Italian bread, about 6 inches in diameter

1 small wheel of Brie (8 ounces), about 4 inches in diameter, chilled

¼ cup apricot preserves or jam, preferably reduced-sugar

1½ teaspoons Amaretto or brandy

2 tablespoons sliced almonds

1 Preheat the oven to 350°F.

2 Using a long serrated knife, cut off and reserve the top third of the bread loaf. Place the bottom of the loaf, cut side up, on a work surface. Using the Brie as a guide, score a circle in the center of the bread. Use a small serrated grapefruit spoon or your fingers to remove enough of the soft bread to form a hollow deep enough to completely encase the wheel of cheese. Save the discarded bread from the center for bread crumbs or another use.

3 In a small bowl, stir together the apricot preserves and Amaretto until well blended.

4 Spray the blade of a long, thin knife with no-stick cooking spray. Carefully cut the cheese in half horizontally. (If the cheese is too soft, freeze just until firm.) Place the bottom half of the cheese, cut side up, inside the loaf. Spread about 3 tablespoons of the preserves in an even layer over the cheese. Set the top of the Brie in place and press gently to sandwich the layers. Use the tip of a sharp knife to score the top of the cheese rind, which is edible, in a criss-cross pattern about ¼ inch deep. Spread the remaining preserves over the top of the cheese.

5 Wrap the loaf in foil and bake for 20 minutes. Carefully remove the foil and sprinkle the almonds over the jam-topped cheese. Bake uncovered for 10 minutes longer, or until the bread is crisp, the cheese is very soft, and the almonds are lightly toasted. During the last 5 minutes, toast the top of the bread in the oven.

6 To serve, place the loaf on a large platter and lean the lid against the bread at an angle. Have guests scoop out the warm cheese with a knife or spoon, for spreading on bread, crackers, or fruit.

baked brie
with cranberry salsa

This two-part appetizer is a study in contrasts: rich, warm oozing cheese is topped with cool, sweet-tart cranberries accentuated with the bite of fresh ginger, the heat of jalapeño, and the refreshing sensation of lime and mint. Serve with plain unsalted crackers, such as water biscuits, or with Crostini (page 119).

► *Serves 10 to 12*

1½ cups (6 ounces) fresh or frozen cranberries

⅓ cup sugar

½ cup lightly packed fresh mint leaves

2 scallions, coarsely chopped

Grated zest and juice of 1 lime

1½ teaspoons grated fresh ginger

1 to 1½ teaspoons seeded and minced fresh jalapeño pepper, to taste

⅛ teaspoon salt

1 (6-inch) wheel of Brie (19.6 ounces)

1 In a food processor, combine the cranberries, sugar, mint, scallions, lime zest and juice, ginger, jalapeño pepper, and salt. Pulse until the cranberries are uniformly chopped and the ingredients are well mixed. Do not overprocess. Transfer the salsa to a small bowl, cover, and refrigerate until the sugar has dissolved and the flavors have blended, at least 1 hour or up to 6 hours.

2 Preheat the oven to 350°F. Place the cheese on a heatproof serving dish and bake for 25 to 30 minutes, until the wheel is soft when touched in the center but still holds its shape.

3 Spoon the chilled salsa over the hot cheese and serve at once.

fiesta chili dip with ground turkey and corn

Hearty layered Mexican dips are always a hit at casual parties. Serve this one as is, or pile on the toppings once it's out of the oven: sour cream, guacamole, sliced ripe olives, pickled jalapeño slices, and chopped fresh cilantro would all be welcome additions. Serve with Baked Tortilla Chips (page 123) or scoop-shaped corn chips.

▶ *Makes about 4 cups; serves 8 to 10*

---

1 tablespoon vegetable oil

1 pound ground turkey

½ teaspoon salt

2 teaspoons chili powder

1 teaspoon ground cumin

1 can (15 ounces) vegetarian chili with beans

1 can (11 ounces) corn kernels, well drained

½ cup thinly sliced scallions

½ cup chunky tomato salsa

1 cup (4 ounces) shredded Mexican cheese blend

1 In a large skillet, heat the oil over medium-high heat. Add the ground turkey and season with the salt. Cook, breaking the meat into small pieces as you stir, until no trace of pink remains, 5 to 7 minutes.

2 Stir in the chili powder and cumin. Add the chili, corn, scallions, and salsa. Cook, stirring occasionally, for 3 minutes. Scrape the mixture into a shallow 1½-quart baking dish. Sprinkle the cheese evenly over the top. (If made in advance, cover with plastic wrap and refrigerate for up to 24 hours.)

3 Preheat the oven to 350°F. Bake, uncovered, for 20 to 25 minutes, until the cheese is melted and the turkey mixture is bubbly hot. Serve warm.

cowboy nacho dip

Cowboy here refers to the pinto beans, *nacho* to the Southwestern flavors involved: namely cheese, jalapeños, salsa, and the corn chips used for dipping. While this is recommended as a hot dip, leftovers can be enjoyed chilled or at room temperature as well.

▶ *Makes about 2 cups; serves 6 to 8*

1 can (15 ounces) pinto beans, rinsed and well drained

1½ cups shredded sharp cheddar cheese (about 6 ounces)

½ cup mild salsa

½ cup sour cream

1 tablespoon taco seasoning mix

2 teaspoons ground cumin

1 teaspoon mashed canned chipotles in adobo sauce

⅓ cup minced scallions

2 teaspoons minced pickled jalapeño peppers

1 In a food processor, combine the pinto beans, cheddar cheese, salsa, sour cream, taco seasoning, cumin, and mashed chipotles. Puree until smooth. Add the scallions and pickled jalapeños and pulse to mix evenly.

2 Transfer to a glass or ceramic serving bowl and microwave for 2 to 3 minutes on high, stopping to stir once halfway through. Or heat gently in a heavy saucepan over low heat. Stir well before serving.

melted cheese
with spicy chorizo

Gooey melted cheese, or *queso fundido* as it's called in Mexico, is always irresistible. Add some spicy sausage and you've got the makings of a great appetizer. Serve this casual spread with warm flour tortillas, corn tortilla chips, or Baked Tortilla Chips (page 123), Salsa Fresca (page 75), and plenty of napkins.

▶ *Serves 4 to 6*

---

8 ounces chorizo or other spicy sausage, removed from casing

2 teaspoons vegetable oil

12 ounces shredded Monterey Jack cheese (about 3 cups)

1 scallion, thinly sliced

1 Preheat the oven to 375°F.

2 Crumble the chorizo into a skillet and cook over medium heat, breaking up the meat into small bits, until fully cooked and nicely browned, about 5 minutes. Remove from the heat. Drain off the fat, leaving the chorizo in the skillet.

3 Grease an 8-inch gratin or other heat-proof dish with the oil. Warm it in the oven for 3 to 4 minutes, until hot. Using a potholder, remove the dish from the oven and sprinkle the cheese evenly over the bottom. Bake for 6 to 8 minutes, or until the cheese is bubbly hot.

4 Meanwhile, reheat the chorizo over medium heat until sizzling, about 2 minutes. Remove the cheese from the oven and scatter the chorizo over the top. Garnish with the sliced scallion. Serve at once right from the baking dish.

baked fontina
with marinated mushrooms

Utterly simple and best shared with close friends huddled around the dish of molten cheese, this is easiest to scoop up with chunks of crusty Italian bread. Italian fontina boasts incomparable nutty flavor, but a good-quality Gruyère or even generic Swiss cheese can be substituted.

► *Serves 4 to 6*

---

1 tablespoon butter, softened

1 jar (6 ounces) marinated mushrooms

8 ounces Italian fontina cheese, sliced

Crusty Italian bread

1 Preheat the oven to 475°F. Generously butter a 9-inch gratin or glass pie dish.

2 Drain the mushrooms, discarding the marinade. Chop the mushrooms coarsely and mound in the center of the prepared baking dish. Arrange overlapping slices of the cheese in concentric circles on top.

3 Bake for 5 minutes, or until the cheese is bubbly hot and lightly browned at the edges. Serve at once, with chunks of bread.

VARIATION:

baked fontina with artichokes Substitute 1 jar (6 to 8 ounces) marinated artichokes for the marinated mushrooms.

mexicali clam dip

Although this dip can be eaten cool just after it is made, baking
highlights the contrast of flavors and textures, and makes the
creaminess seem more luxurious. Serve with thick potato chips,
Baked Tortilla Chips (page 123), or Baked Pita Chips (page 124).

▶ *Makes 2 cups; serves 8 to 10*

---

2 cans (6½ ounces
each) minced clams

1 package (8 ounces)
cream cheese, cut into
pieces, at room
temperature

¼ teaspoon hot pepper
sauce, such as Tabasco

⅔ cup drained Salsa
Fresca (page 75) or
other chunky tomato
salsa

2 teaspoons chopped
cilantro

1 Preheat the oven to 350°F.

2 Drain the clams, reserving 2 tablespoons of the juice. In a medium bowl,
combine the reserved clam juice, cream
cheese, and hot sauce and mix until smooth.
Stir in the salsa.

3 Transfer the dip to a small baking dish.
Bake for about 25 minutes or until the
dip is heated through. Sprinkle cilantro over
the top and serve at once, right from the
baking dish.

goat cheese marinara
with shredded basil

Three simple ingredients yield triple the flavor you'd expect in this simple spread. Serve with baguette slices, crackers, Rosemary Focaccia (page 120), or Crostini (page 119).

▶ *Serves 4 to 6*

1 small log (5 ounces) of soft white goat cheese (*chèvre*)

1 cup marinara sauce

4 large basil leaves

1 Preheat the oven to 400°F.

2 Cut the goat cheese into rounds about ½ inch thick. Arrange the slices in a single layer in a 2-cup gratin or other small baking dish. Spoon the marinara sauce over the cheese.

3 Bake until the sauce is bubbly hot and the cheese has softened but still holds its shape, 10 to 15 minutes.

4 Stack the basil leaves on top of each other and roll lengthwise into a tight cylinder. Cut crosswise into thin slices. Scatter the basil over the hot marinara sauce and serve at once.

deviled shrimp
with bacon

This tasty mix has a nice little kick that offsets the richness of the other ingredients. Serve with crackers, Baked Pita Chips (page 124), Won Ton Crisps (page 121), or Crostini (page 119) and a colorful array of crudités.

▶ *Makes about 2 cups; serves 6 to 8*

---

8 ounces uncooked medium shrimp in the shell

6 ounces lean thick-sliced bacon

8 ounces cream cheese, at room temperature

½ cup mayonnaise

⅓ cup freshly grated Parmesan cheese

1½ teaspoons prepared white horseradish

1 teaspoon fresh lemon juice

⅛ teaspoon cayenne pepper

3 scallions, thinly sliced

1 Preheat the oven to 375°F.

2 Bring a large saucepan of salted water to a boil over high heat. Add the shrimp and cook just until pink and slightly curled, 1½ to 2 minutes. Drain and rinse under cold water. When cool enough to handle, peel and devein the shrimp. Chop coarsely.

3 In a large skillet, cook the bacon over medium heat until nicely browned, 5 to 7 minutes. Drain on paper towels, then chop finely.

4 In a medium bowl, combine the cream cheese, mayonnaise, all but 1 tablespoon of the Parmesan cheese, the horseradish, lemon juice, and cayenne. Mix until well blended. Stir in the shrimp, bacon, and scallions. Scrape the mixture into a small gratin or other shallow baking dish, spreading into an even layer. Sprinkle the remaining 1 tablespoon of Parmesan over the top.

5 Bake for about 20 minutes, until the mixture is bubbly hot and the top is lightly browned. Serve warm, right from the baking dish.

warm sweet and sour dip

Great for dipping cocktail meatballs, mini sausages, and Won Ton Crisps (page 121), this easy classic sauce has been updated with fresh ginger and lemon for added zest. If made ahead, reheat gently before serving; the sauce is best warm rather than hot.

▶ *Makes about 2 cups; serves 10 to 12*

1 bottle (12 ounces) chili sauce

1 jar (8 ounces) grape jelly

2 teaspoons finely grated fresh ginger

1 teaspoon soy sauce

2 tablespoons fresh lemon juice

1 In a small saucepan, combine the chili sauce, grape jelly, ginger, and soy sauce. Cook over medium heat, stirring occasionally, until heated through, 2 to 3 minutes. Remove from the heat and stir in the lemon juice.

2 Serve at once, or cover and refrigerate for up to 3 days. Warm over low heat or in a microwave before serving.

warm olive pizza dip

Kalamata olives add a lot of flavor, and if you buy them already pitted, this recipe will take no time at all. You could also add any of your favorite pizza toppings, such as sautéed chopped mushrooms, bell peppers, onions; cooked and crumbled Italian sausage; or even diced pepperoni. Serve with baguette slices, Garlic Crostini (page 119), breadsticks, Rosemary Focaccia (page 120), or crisp vegetables like broccoli, fennel, or celery.

▶ *Makes about 2¼ cups; serves 8 to 10*

---

1 jar (16 ounces) pizza sauce

6 ounces cream cheese, cut into pieces, at room temperature

½ cup coarsely chopped pitted kalamata olives

¼ cup freshly grated Parmesan cheese

3 tablespoons chopped oil-packed sun-dried tomatoes

1 teaspoon Italian seasoning blend

½ teaspoon balsamic vinegar

1 In a medium saucepan, combine the pizza sauce and cream cheese. Cook over medium-low heat, whisking until smooth.

2 Stir in the olives, Parmesan cheese, sun-dried tomatoes, Italian seasoning, and balsamic vinegar. Cook for 3 to 5 minutes, or until heated through.

3 Transfer to a bowl and serve at once. Alternatively, transfer to a small fondue pot or chafing dish. Regulate the heat under the pot, if possible, so the dip remains warm, not hot.

chile con queso

Scoff if you like, but there is simply no substitute for Velveeta® in this authentically flavored Tex-Mex favorite. It melts perfectly and provides just the right creamy consistency and mellow flavor. By using mild salsa, you can control the heat with the amount of pickled jalapeños you add. Serve in a ceramic fondue pot or chafing dish, with corn tortilla chips, cooked cocktail sausages or wieners, and cherry tomatoes or other fresh vegetables for dipping.

► *Makes about 3 cups; serves 8 to 10*

---

1 teaspoon cumin seeds (see Note)

1 pound Velveeta, cut into small cubes

¼ cup milk

½ cup shredded sharp cheddar cheese

1 can (4 ounces) chopped mild green chiles

¼ cup mild salsa

1 teaspoon minced pickled jalapeño peppers, or more to taste

1 In a small dry skillet, toast the cumin seeds over medium heat, tossing occasionally, until they are fragrant and slightly darkened, about 3 minutes. Transfer to a mortar and crush lightly.

2 In a medium saucepan, combine the Velveeta and milk. Cook over low heat, covered, until the milk is hot and the Velveeta melts, about 5 minutes. Add the cheddar cheese and cook until melted, about 2 minutes longer.

3 Add the chiles, salsa, pickled jalapeño peppers, and toasted cumin seeds. Stir to mix well. Simmer for about 3 minutes longer to allow the flavors to develop.

4 Transfer to a fondue pot or chafing dish and serve at once. Regulate the heat under the pot, if possible, so that the dip remains warm, not hot.

NOTE: To save a bit of time, you can skip step 1 and add ½ teaspoon ground cumin in step 3, but it will not have quite the same flavor as freshly toasted seeds.

crab amandine dip

A blanket of crunchy toasted almonds makes a perfect counterpoint to the rich crab dip that lies beneath. For larger parties, this favorite standby recipe is easily doubled. It tastes delicious with just about anything, though you can never go wrong with baguette slices, Crostini (page 119), Baked Pita Chips (page 124), broccoli spears, and baby carrots.

► *Makes about 2 cups; serves 8 to 10*

8 ounces cream cheese, at room temperature

2 tablespoons mayonnaise

1½ tablespoons dry white wine or vermouth

½ teaspoon prepared white horseradish

¼ teaspoon salt

⅛ teaspoon hot pepper sauce, such as Tabasco

8 ounces lump crabmeat, picked over to remove any bits of shell or cartilage and well drained

2 tablespoons minced fresh chives

¼ cup sliced almonds

1 Preheat the oven to 375°F.

2 In a medium bowl, combine the cream cheese, mayonnaise, wine, horseradish, salt, and hot sauce. Mix until well blended. Fold in the crab and chives. Transfer to a small gratin or other shallow baking dish and sprinkle the almonds over the top.

3 Bake for 15 minutes, or until the almonds are lightly browned and the crab mixture is bubbling hot.

dependable
dunkers

bagel chips 118
golden bagel chips 118
crostini 119
garlic crostini 119
rosemary focaccia 120
won ton crisps 121
parmesan won ton crisps 121
sesame won ton crisps 121
spiced won ton crisps 121
poppadums 122
baked tortilla chips 123
golden baked chips 123
spiced baked chips 123
baked pita chips 124
cheesy pita chips 124
golden pita chips 124
herbed pita chips 124
spiced pita chips 124

bagel chips

Everyone loves fresh bagels, but commercially produced bagel chips can be dry and tasteless. For the best of both worlds, give this recipe a try with any of your favorite flavor of bagels.

▶ *Makes about 48 chips*

---

3 bagels

1 Preheat the oven to 325°F.

2 Using a long serrated knife, cut each bagel in half crosswise, making 2 half-circles. Working one at a time, stand a bagel half cut side down on a work surface. Carefully slice as thinly as possible, getting about 8 slices per bagel half.

3 Arrange the slices in a single layer on 1 or 2 large baking sheets. Bake until crisp and lightly browned at the edges, 5 to 7 minutes. Serve slightly warm or at room temperature. These chips are best served the same day they are made.

VARIATION

golden bagel chips Brush the top of each bagel slice with olive oil or spray with no-stick cooking spray and bake until lightly browned, 6 to 8 minutes.

crostini

Fresh baguettes are great to serve with dips and spreads, but they require last-minute slicing that is a nuisance when you're entertaining. These little toasts make a deliciously crunchy base for cheeses and other spreads and can be easily prepared in advance.

▶ *Makes about 50 crostini*

---

1 baguette (8 to 12 ounces), sliced ¼ to ⅜ inch thick

⅓ cup extra-virgin olive oil

1 Preheat the oven to 400°F.

2 Arrange the bread slices in a single layer on a large baking sheet. Brush the top of each slice lightly with oil.

3 Bake for 7 to 10 minutes, until golden and lightly toasted at the edges. Let cool. Use at once, or store airtight at room temperature for up to 3 days.

VARIATION

garlic crostini Bake the crostini as directed above. When cool enough to handle, rub the browned side of each with the cut side of a garlic clove, grating against the rough surface to distribute the garlic flavor.

rosemary focaccia

Bite-size squares of fragrant flat bread slicked with olive oil make a nice addition to any bread basket. This one begins with frozen bread dough, so it couldn't be easier.

▶ *Makes 1 loaf, about 11 by 7 inches; serves 6 to 8*

---

2 tablespoons chopped fresh rosemary or 2 teaspoons chopped dried

1 loaf (1 pound) frozen bread dough, thawed

3 tablespoons extra-virgin olive oil

2 teaspoons yellow cornmeal

½ teaspoon kosher or other coarse salt

1 On a lightly floured work surface, knead the rosemary into the dough. Let rest for 5 minutes.

2 Brush an 11 by 7-inch baking pan with 1 tablespoon of the olive oil and sprinkle with the cornmeal. Pat or roll out the bread dough to fit inside the pan. Brush the surface of the dough with 1 tablespoon of the olive oil and sprinkle with salt. Indent the surface of the dough by pressing all over with your fingertips. Cover with a kitchen towel and let rise in a warm, draft-free spot for 1 hour, or until nicely puffed but not necessarily doubled in bulk. Press the dough again all over with your fingertips.

3 Meanwhile, preheat the oven to 375°F. Brush the dough with the remaining 1 tablespoon olive oil. Bake for 18 to 20 minutes, or until the bread is baked through and the top is golden brown. Let cool for 5 minutes in the pan, then transfer to a wire rack. Serve slightly warm or at room temperature, cut into small squares. This is best served the same day it is made.

won ton crisps

Won ton wrappers are usually sold in 1-pound packages, either refrigerated or frozen. Each package contains anywhere from 80 to 120 wrappers, depending upon their thickness. When cut diagonally into 2 triangles, wrappers make crispy bite-size chips for dips. For a more whimsical approach, won tons can be wrinkled and baked in irregular shapes: just scrunch them in your hand and place on a baking sheet prior to brushing and baking.

▶ *Makes 48*

---

24 won ton wrappers (about 3 inches square)

¼ cup olive oil or melted butter

1 Preheat the oven to 350°F.

2 Stack the won ton wrappers and using a large sharp knife, cut in half diagonally to make triangular pieces. Line a baking sheet with foil to facilitate cleanup. Arrange the wrappers in a single layer so the edges are not touching. Brush with oil.

3 Bake for 6 to 8 minutes, until lightly golden and crisp. Let cool on a wire rack. Serve at once or store in an airtight container for up to 3 days.

VARIATIONS

parmesan won ton crisps After brushing with oil or butter, sprinkle 3 to 4 tablespoons freshly grated Parmesan cheese over the wrappers and season with freshly ground black pepper to taste. Bake as directed above.

sesame won ton crisps Instead of olive oil or butter, lightly brush the wrappers with 3 tablespoons Asian sesame oil and sprinkle with 2 tablespoons black or white sesame seeds. Bake as directed above.

spiced won ton crisps After brushing with olive oil or butter, sprinkle the wrappers very lightly with a spice such as curry powder, chili powder, or hot paprika. Bake as directed above.

poppadums

These savory crisp lentil wafers puff up dramatically in hot oil. Poppadums are delightful on their own or as a vehicle for delivering chutneys and other dips. Look for them in Indian grocery stores and in the ethnic foods section of gourmet supermarkets. They come plain or spiced, with flavors like cumin, pepper, garlic, or chile.

▶ *Makes about 15*

2 to 4 cups peanut or vegetable oil

1 box or bag (4 ounces) plain or spiced poppadums, about 5 inches in diameter

1 In a large wok or skillet, heat the oil to 375°F on a deep-frying thermometer. Using tongs, slide the poppadums into the hot oil one at a time. Fry, turning once if needed, until the poppadums are puffed and golden, 4 to 5 seconds.

2 Drain well on paper towels, and blot gently to absorb excess oil. Serve the whole poppadums warm or at room temperature. Have guests break off pieces for dipping.

baked tortilla chips

Latin markets sometimes carry a rainbow of fresh tortillas—made with dusky red chili powder, blue cornmeal, or earthy whole wheat flour. While bagged chips are convenient, homemade have incomparable taste and texture.

▶ *Makes 48 tortilla chips*

---

8 corn or flour tortillas, about 6 inches round

1 Preheat the oven to 400°F.

2 Stack the tortillas on top of each other and cut into 6 pie-shaped wedges. Alternatively, cut the tortillas into strips or irregularly shaped, elongated triangles. Lay the tortilla wedges flat in a single layer on one or more baking sheets.

3 Bake for 5 minutes. Turn over and bake for 5 minutes longer, or until crisp. Let cool. If made in advance, store in an airtight container at room temperature for up to 2 days.

VARIATIONS

golden baked chips Before baking, lightly brush each tortilla wedge with vegetable or olive oil, or spray with no-stick cooking spray.

spiced baked chips After brushing with oil, sprinkle the tortilla wedges very lightly with a spice such as coarse salt, chili powder, or cumin. Bake as directed above.

baked pita chips

Pocket bread makes delicious crispy, low-fat chips to serve with dips and spreads. The pita triangles take on a natural curl as they bake, making them attractive as well as practical. Serve them plain, or seasoned as suggested in the variations below.

▶ *Makes 48 pita chips*

---

4 white or whole wheat pita pocket breads (6 to 7 inches in diameter)

1 Preheat the oven to 400°F.

2 Split the pita breads horizontally to make 8 rounds. Stack the rounds on top of each other and cut into 6 pie-shaped wedges. Lay the pita wedges flat in a single layer on one or more baking sheets.

3 Bake until crisp and barely browned at the edges, 7 to 10 minutes. Let cool. If made in advance, store in an airtight container at room temperature for up to 2 days.

VARIATIONS

cheesy pita chips Before baking, sprinkle the rough side of each pita triangle with freshly grated Parmesan cheese.

golden pita chips Before baking, lightly brush the rough side of each pita triangle with plain or flavored extra-virgin olive oil, such as garlic, basil, or lemon oil; or spray with no-stick cooking spray.

herbed pita chips Before baking, lightly brush the rough side of each pita triangle with extra-virgin olive oil and sprinkle with a dash of dried herbs or spices, such as dill or crushed fennel seed.

spiced pita chips Before baking, lightly brush the rough side of each pita triangle with extra-virgin olive oil and sprinkle lightly with a mix of coarse salt and zahtar, a Middle Eastern blend of sesame seeds, powdered sumac, and dried thyme, or with a mix of coarse salt, cumin, and cayenne pepper or chipotle chile powder.

index